Catholic Mother Goose

by Leane VanderPutten

Pencil Drawings by
Becky Melechinsky
&
Virginia Shibler

Graphic Illustration by
Leane VanderPutten

DEDICATION

I dedicate this book
to all the Catholic mothers
striving to give
the gift of Catholic culture
to their families.

FOREWORD

Who can resist those little ditties, those lovely little sing-song verses called Nursery Rhymes! Songs and rhymes for young children have been passed down from generation to generation. They are fun, children love them, and they provide a warm, nurturing experience for the whole family.

Nursery Rhymes can be very valuable in a child's reading development. They are short and easy to repeat and they become some of the child's first sentences. They also help the child practice the rhythm of language....pitch, volume and voice inflection.

Our own children grew up learning and repeating Nursery Rhymes. It was very enjoyable and it was an easy way to teach the children the use of rhythm and rhyme. How much more meaningful those little poems would have been if there had been more depth in the considerations behind each little verse!

That is where this book comes in. It gives us some lovely rhymes that can, and should, be committed to heart by your children. Not only will it provide all the benefits of reading and memorizing, but it will supply some simple reflections that will turn those little minds to what is most important in their life....their Catholic Faith.

It is important that young children learn to memorize through verse.

Research shows children learn more in their first eight years than they do in the rest of their lives. This is a powerful time to teach them.

So, parents, here is a teaching tool that can help! Encourage your children to learn the poems in this book. Let them peruse the pages and look at the pictures. You will find that it will be a meaningful experience for all!

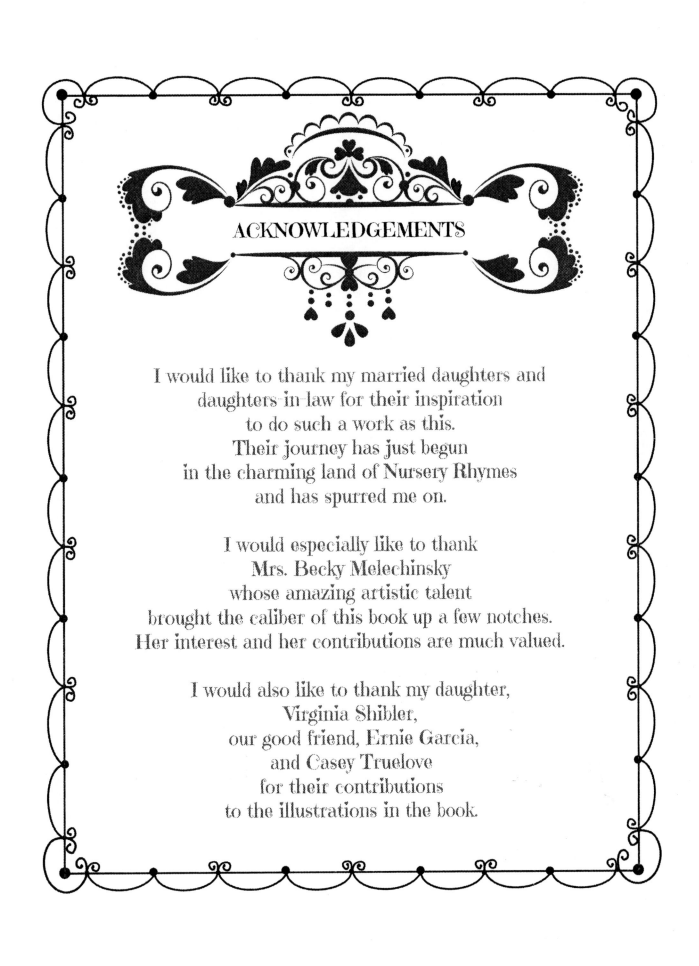

ACKNOWLEDGEMENTS

I would like to thank my married daughters and
daughters-in-law for their inspiration
to do such a work as this.
Their journey has just begun
in the charming land of Nursery Rhymes
and has spurred me on.

I would especially like to thank
Mrs. Becky Melechinsky
whose amazing artistic talent
brought the caliber of this book up a few notches.
Her interest and her contributions are much valued.

I would also like to thank my daughter,
Virginia Shibler,
our good friend, Ernie Garcia,
and Casey Truelove
for their contributions
to the illustrations in the book.

Table of Contents

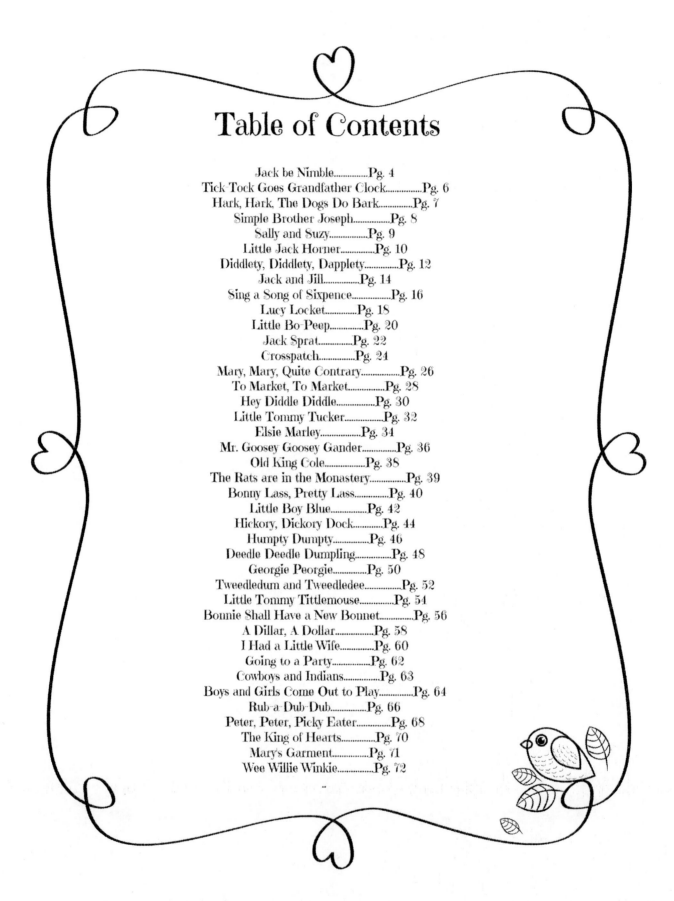

Jack be Nimble............Pg. 4
Tick Tock Goes Grandfather Clock............Pg. 6
Hark, Hark, The Dogs Do Bark............Pg. 7
Simple Brother Joseph............Pg. 8
Sally and Suzy............Pg. 9
Little Jack Horner............Pg. 10
Diddlety, Diddlety, Dapplety............Pg. 12
Jack and Jill............Pg. 14
Sing a Song of Sixpence............Pg. 16
Lucy Locket............Pg. 18
Little Bo-Peep............Pg. 20
Jack Sprat............Pg. 22
Crosspatch............Pg. 24
Mary, Mary, Quite Contrary............Pg. 26
To Market, To Market............Pg. 28
Hey Diddle Diddle............Pg. 30
Little Tommy Tucker............Pg. 32
Elsie Marley............Pg. 34
Mr. Goosey Goosey Gander............Pg. 36
Old King Cole............Pg. 38
The Rats are in the Monastery............Pg. 39
Bonny Lass, Pretty Lass............Pg. 40
Little Boy Blue............Pg. 42
Hickory, Dickory Dock............Pg. 44
Humpty Dumpty............Pg. 46
Deedle Deedle Dumpling............Pg. 48
Georgie Peorgie............Pg. 50
Tweedledum and Tweedledee............Pg. 52
Little Tommy Tittlemouse............Pg. 54
Bonnie Shall Have a New Bonnet............Pg. 56
A Dillar, A Dollar............Pg. 58
I Had a Little Wife............Pg. 60
Going to a Party............Pg. 62
Cowboys and Indians............Pg. 63
Boys and Girls Come Out to Play............Pg. 64
Rub-a-Dub-Dub............Pg. 66
Peter, Peter, Picky Eater............Pg. 68
The King of Hearts............Pg. 70
Mary's Garment............Pg. 71
Wee Willie Winkie............Pg. 72

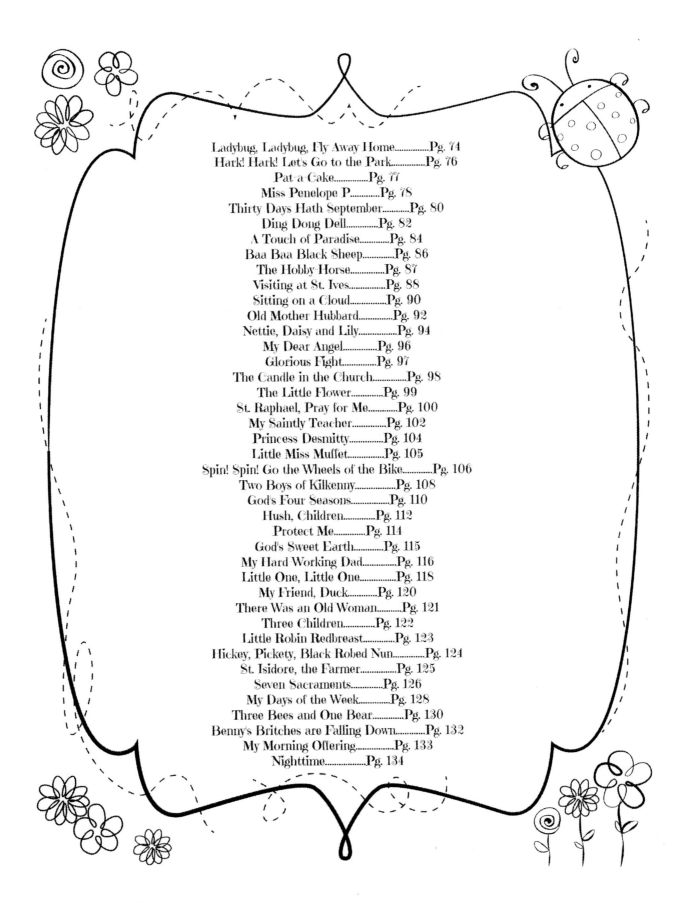

Ladybug, Ladybug, Fly Away Home..............Pg. 74

Hark! Hark! Let's Go to the Park..............Pg. 76

Pat-a-Cake..............Pg. 77

Miss Penelope P..............Pg. 78

Thirty Days Hath September..............Pg. 80

Ding Dong Dell..............Pg. 82

A Touch of Paradise..............Pg. 84

Baa Baa Black Sheep..............Pg. 86

The Hobby-Horse..............Pg. 87

Visiting at St. Ives..............Pg. 88

Sitting on a Cloud..............Pg. 90

Old Mother Hubbard..............Pg. 92

Nettie, Daisy and Lily..............Pg. 94

My Dear Angel..............Pg. 96

Glorious Fight..............Pg. 97

The Candle in the Church..............Pg. 98

The Little Flower..............Pg. 99

St. Raphael, Pray for Me..............Pg. 100

My Saintly Teacher..............Pg. 102

Princess Desmitty..............Pg. 104

Little Miss Muffet..............Pg. 105

Spin! Spin! Go the Wheels of the Bike..............Pg. 106

Two Boys of Kilkenny..............Pg. 108

God's Four Seasons..............Pg. 110

Hush, Children..............Pg. 112

Protect Me..............Pg. 114

God's Sweet Earth..............Pg. 115

My Hard Working Dad..............Pg. 116

Little One, Little One..............Pg. 118

My Friend, Duck..............Pg. 120

There Was an Old Woman..............Pg. 121

Three Children..............Pg. 122

Little Robin Redbreast..............Pg. 123

Hickey, Pickety, Black Robed Nun..............Pg. 124

St. Isidore, the Farmer..............Pg. 125

Seven Sacraments..............Pg. 126

My Days of the Week..............Pg. 128

Three Bees and One Bear..............Pg. 130

Benny's Britches are Falling Down..............Pg. 132

My Morning Offering..............Pg. 133

Nighttime..............Pg. 134

Jack Be Nimble

Jack be Nimble, Jack be quick;
Jack go light the candlestick.
It's time to kneel, it's time to pray;
We say our rosary every day!

Jack be nimble, Jack be quick;
Jack go light the candlestick.
Young altar boy, it's time for Mass;
Say your Latin, but not too fast!

Tick-Tock Goes Grandfather Clock

Tick-Tock goes Grandfather Clock;
Majestic and Grand by the wall.
Tick-Tock, it seems it can talk;
Winking at me in the hall.

Tick-Tock, it says to take stock,
As time is marching on by.
Tick-Tock, reminds Grandfather Clock;
Be ready for when I die!

Tick-Tock, goes Grandfather Clock,
As we get closer to our reward.
Before you know it, we'll be there,
To see Mary and Our Lord!

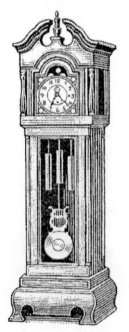

Hark, Hark, The Dogs Do Bark

Hark! hark! the dogs do bark,
The poor man is coming to town;
We hear him sigh, we see him limp
We see his very sad frown.

We sit him down, we give him bread
He's happy now because he's fed.
We're happy too because we shared
And showed the man that Jesus cares.

Simple Brother Joseph

Simple Joseph, didn't know much;
But he had lots of spunk.
Cheerful Joseph, loved God so much;
He became a monk.

In his habit, came the Abbot;
Brother Joseph for to see;
He was put in charge, of the monks at large;
Joseph did it willingly.

The monks didn't grumble, for Joseph was humble;
There never was a complaint.
The place became known, for its holiness alone;
And Brother Joseph became a saint.

Sally and Suzy

Sally and Suzy are two little girls:
The alarm clock rang, they were up in a whirl!
Suzy hugged Sally; she began to say,
"Oh, Sister Sally, today's the big day!
We'll don our gown and put on our veil;
Our Lord we'll receive at the Communion Rail!"

Little Jack Horner

Little Jack Horner sat in the corner,
Because he'd been naughty that day.
He repented his sin,
Kissed his mom on the chin;
For his penance he said an "Ave".

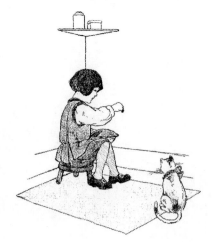

Diddlety, Diddlety, Dapplety

Diddlety, diddlety, dapplety,
Sue's sitting under the apple tree,
Reading her missal,
On St. Paul's epistle,
Diddlety, diddlety, dapplety.

Diddlety, diddlety, dapplety,
Sue went to visit the chapel with me.
We said a small prayer,
Strolled home without care,
Diddlety, diddlety, dapplety.

Jack and Jill

Jack and Jill
Looked up the hill,
And thought of Jesus dying.
He had died
Because of our pride;
It made them feel like crying.

Jack and Jill,
With much goodwill,
Went to the church to pray.
They prayed for those,
Who are Jesus' foes;
And promised they'd be
good each day!

Sing a Song of Sixpence

Sing a song of sixpence,
Let's take it to the store;
To get some juicy apples
For in the pie to pour.

Today's the special feast day
Of Jesus Christ, our King!
We'll have a small procession;
We will pray and we will sing.

Let's don our special clothes
And march around the lawn;
Then all meet in the parlor,
The chairs we'll sit upon.

Kate will serve the pie,
John will serve the punch;
We'll say our little grace
And enjoy our lovely lunch!

Lucy Locket

Lucy Locket, tore her pocket,
Kitty sewed it well;
Now each lass, will walk to Mass,
Where Our Lord does dwell.

Little Bo-Peep

Little Bo-Peep has lost her sheep,
And doesn't know where to find them.
She runs and climbs, and falls at times;
She's hoping she's right behind them!

Little Bo-Peep has found her sheep;
She rejoices all through the day!
Their location revealed, they're back in the field;
Skipping and jumping at play!

Jesus doesn't sleep, He's also lost sheep;
He loves them until they come home.
He's very gentle, and not judgmental;
But He teaches them not to roam.

Jesus doesn't weep, He's found **HIS** sheep;
They've come home to Him for good.
They pray to their Queen, to keep their souls clean;
And love Jesus just as they should!

Jack Sprat

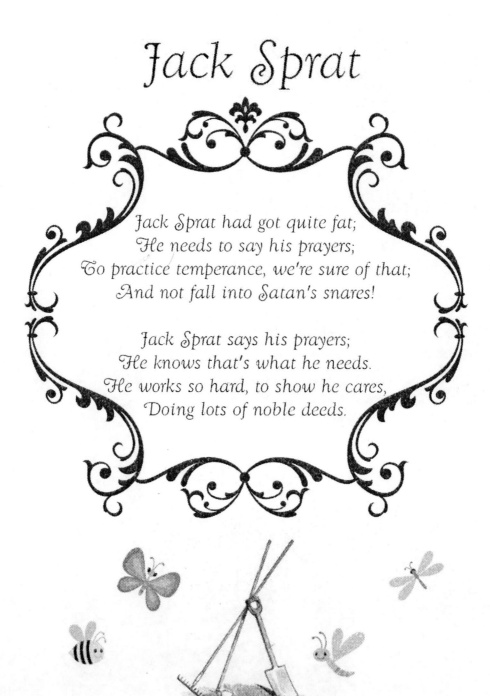

Jack Sprat had got quite fat;
He needs to say his prayers;
To practice temperance, we're sure of that;
And not fall into Satan's snares!

Jack Sprat says his prayers;
He knows that's what he needs.
He works so hard, to show he cares,
Doing lots of noble deeds.

Crosspatch

Crosspatch, you must detach;
Share with your brother today.
No more mumbling, if you stop
grumbling,
With your game you may play!

Mary, Mary, Quite Contrary

Mary, Mary, quite contrary,
Turn to Our Lady, do not
tarry!
She'll help you with your
attitude;
Making it love and
gratitude.

To Market, To Market

To market, to market, it's
now time to bake,
Home again, home again, a
little plum cake;
It's Our Lady's day, let's feast
and be merry!
She'll help us be good and
our burdens she'll carry.

Hey Diddle, Diddle

Hey Diddle Diddle,
Let's take out our fiddle,
Turn out a tune or two.
We'll frolic and dance,
We'll skip and we'll prance;
Our friends will join in, too!

Hey Diddle Diddle,
Put away our fiddle,
For the rosary we will pray.
We'll kneel up straight,
Even though it's late;
The best way to end our day!

Little Tommy Tucker

Little Tommy Tucker prays before his supper,
That is how he thanks God for his bread and butter.
Now he cuts it carefully, with his little knife;
And thanks God again, for his happy little life!

Bless us, O Lord, and
these Thy gifts...

Elsie Marley

Elsie Marley has grown so
haughty,
She's always complaining and
really quite naughty;
She'll go to confession and
make her soul white;
She'll try to be good, with all of
her might!

Mr. Goosey Goosey Gander

Mr. Goosey Goosey Gander,
Tell me where do you meander?
Are you going for a little chat
With pleasant Mr. Thomas Cat?

As you pass the church, Good Chap,
Don't forget to tip your cap.
Jesus is waiting there for you;
So stop to say a prayer or two.

You will smile and keep on walking,
Meeting friends and gaily talking.
Others like you for your candor,
Mr. Goosey Goosey Gander!

Virginia Shibler

37

Old King Cole

Old King Cole had a grace-filled soul;
A kindly old ruler was he.
He called for his knight,
He called for his queen,
And he called for his sons, all three.

Old King Cole, he wanted a feast;
He invited the poor and depraved.
His palace was full,
Their stomachs were too;
Not a single one misbehaved!

Old King Cole, it was time to die;
His soul flew straight to heaven!
God's arms were open,
To receive him in;
Knowing what King Cole had given!

The Rats are in the Monastery

The rats are in the monastery,
What are the brothers to do?
They're running hither and dither,
Even when the monks say, "Shoo!"

They're getting into the closets;
They're scampering through the rooms!
The monks are feeling desperate,
As they hit them with their brooms!

St. Martin de Porres will help them;
He'll tell them to all go away!
He calls the rodents to order,
In his quiet, gentle way.

He tells them they must go;
He'll feed them every day.
They march right out the door,
And in the barn they stay.

Ernest Garcia

Bonny Lass, Pretty Lass

Bonny lass, pretty lass, your beauty doth
shine;
Your faith is so pure, your goodness so
fine.
You'd make a good mother, you'd make a
fine wife;
I dream I may one day share your life.

Bonny lass, pretty lass, wilt thou be mine?
We shall be happy, as our lives intertwine.
We'll love our children, and teach them
their prayers,
We'll love Our Lord, and give Him our
cares.

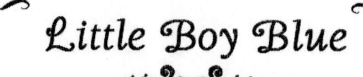

Little Boy Blue

Little Boy Blue, come blow your horn,
It is time for Mass, this early morn.
No more sleeping upon the hay;
Don your jacket, and do not stray!

Little Boy Blue, don't blow your horn;
We shall be quiet at Mass this morn.
For now it's time for consecration;
Look to Him who helps with temptation.

Little Boy Blue now blow your horn;
Since Mass is over I don't have to warn.
You've received God, your heart says "Hooray!"
You can go back to playing today!

Hickory, Dickory Dock

Hickory, Dickory, Dock
Jesus at the door will knock.
He wants into your heart,
His love He'll impart,
Hickory, Dickory, Dock.

Hickory, Dickory, Doo
He's waiting there for you.
You open the door,
He waits there no more;
He's in your heart loving
you!

45

Humpty Dumpty

Humpty Dumpty wouldn't study at all;
So Humpty Dumpty jumped over the
wall!
He tried to skip school, he was being a
fool!
Did he want his brain to stay small?

Humpty Dumpty woke up to his folly;
Humpty Dumpty did better, by golly!
He studied a lot, good grades he got,
He felt better, and became quite jolly!

Deedle Deedle Dumpling

Deedle Deedle
Dumpling my son, Todd,
Plopped into bed without
talking to God.
As he was drifting off to
sleep,
He remembered and out
of bed did leap!
He asked Jesus his soul
to keep;
And fell back into a nice,
deep sleep.

Georgie Peorgie

Georgie Peorgie was a real wise guy;
He loved to tease, till the girls would cry.
He'd dangle live snakes, just to horrify;
Georgie was naughty and really quite sly!

Georgie Peorgie was doing his tricks,
He saw Father and his conscience he pricks.
He went to church, looked at the crucifix;
Then went to confession, his soul to fix.

Tweedledum and Tweedledee

Tweedledum and Tweedledee
Went out in the yard one day.
Said Tweedledum to Tweedledee,
"Let's climb a tree and play!"

Said Tweedledee to Tweedledum,
"I can't, I lost my shoe!"
Said Tweedledum to Tweedledee,
"St. Anthony will care for you."

Both the brothers made their plea
To the good, kind St. Anthony.
They saw the shoe under the tree;
No more barefoot Tweedledee!

Little Tommy Tittlemouse

In the church there is a tiny house,
Where lives Tommy Tittlemouse.

At half past nine the bell is pealing;
We peek in and see him kneeling.

Every day at half past four,
He cleans the crumbs upon the floor.

Every night at half past eight,
He says his prayers because it's late.

Little Tommy Tittlemouse
Loves his special little house!

Bonnie Shall Have a New Bonnet

Bonnie shall have a new bonnet,
For soon it will be Easter morn.
She'll go to the Holy Week Service;
At the Vigil her bonnet adorn.

She'll don her pretty new dress,
On this great and lovely day!
With peace she'll prepare her heart;
For Jesus to come and stay!

A Dillar, A Dollar

A dillar, a dollar,
Let's straighten our collar;
Our pennies we have saved.
We'll go to Mass, the basket's passed;
We're happy that we gave!

A dillar, a dollar,
We're feeling much taller;
For we've given alms today!
We'll go home and change our clothes;
And with our friends we'll play!

I Had a Little Wife

I had a little wife,
The loveliest ever seen.
She feeds me healthy dinners
And keeps the house so clean.

She grinds the wheat each day
And then she bakes the bread.
She sews up all my trousers
With her needle and her thread.

Every day she says her prayers;
I watch her as she kneels.
She doesn't know I'm peeking
At the moments that she steals!

I love my little wife,
I'm thankful for her care.
I work for her each day
And lift her up in prayer!

Going to a Party

Hey biddle pinkety boppety-doo;
I'm getting ready for a party at two.
I'll put on my dress, so modest and sweet;
I don my socks, my shoes on my feet.
My Miraculous Medal is under my clothes;
Our Lady goes with me wherever I go.
Hey biddle pinkety boppety-doo;
I am leaving now; goodbye, toodle-oo.

Cowboys and Indians

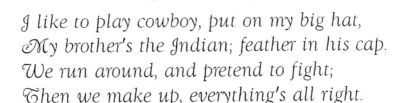

I like to play cowboy, put on my big hat,
My brother's the Indian; feather in his cap.
We run around, and pretend to fight;
Then we make up, everything's all right.

We remember that great St. Isaac Jogues;
He loved the Indians, even his foes.
He converted their hearts, baptized so many;
Communions each day, confessions a-plenty!

Jesus loves all, be they black, red or white;
We should love too; always be polite.
Like Isaac Jogues, that saint of old;
We share our faith, so brave and bold!

Boys and Girls Come Out to Play
-Becky Melechinsky

Boys and girls, come out to play,
The moon doth shine, as if to say,
Our Mother Mary, sweet and mild,
Shines down her love on every child.

Come celebrate the beauteous sight
Of Mary's love, so pure and bright.
Yes, sing and play and laugh, but pray
That we be safe, both night and day.

Oh, pray, this moonlit night, that we
Will safe in Heaven some day be;
And thank the Father, Who , on high,
Didst put the bright moon in the sky.

Rub-a-Dub-Dub

Rub-a-dub-dub, My body I scrub,
To make it as white as snow!
Rub-a-dub-doo, My soul I clean, too;
So off to confession I go!

Rub-a-dub-dee, Jesus cleansed me;
My penance I will say.
Rub-a-dub-doe, The graces do flow;
Now for my priest I will pray!

Peter, Peter, Picky Eater

Peter, Peter, Picky Eater,
Always looking for something sweeter!
Eating treats throughout the day,
Makes you weak, too tired to play!

Peter, Peter, Picky Eater,
Eat your lunch and nothing sweeter!
Deny yourself all day long,
Then your muscles will grow so strong!

The King of Hearts

The King of Hearts, His care imparts
Every single day.
The Spirit of Love, coming from above,
Will guide us on our way.

The Son of Man, He has a plan
For every one of us.
Great Trinity, please smile on me;
Our life we do entrust!

Mary's Garment

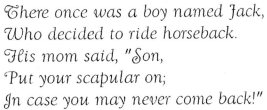

There once was a boy named Jack,
Who decided to ride horseback.
His mom said, "Son,
Put your scapular on;
In case you may never come back!"

This obedient boy named Jack,
Put his scapular upon his back.
Mom's worries ceased,
She was at peace;
For Mary's garment was now upon Jack!

Wee Willie Winkie

Wee Willie Winkie goes thru the town,
Doing good deeds with ne'er a frown;
Helping all the children, a smile upon his face;
Everyone loves him, his heart is full of grace!

Sally scrapes her leg, Willie's right there!
He bandages her sore, with joyful care!
Tommy's bike is broke, Willie's got the tool,
To fix it right up, now Tommy rides to school!

Wee Willie Winkie, gets sick one day;
All the town gathers, so they can pray.
They ask that their frend be healed this day;
Jesus hears their prayers, Willie's okay!

73

Ladybug, Ladybug, Fly Away Home

Ladybug Ladybug, fly away home
Why do you always go out and roam?
Your duties await you, your dishes are dirty;
Ladybug, Ladybug, it's almost ten thirty!

Ladybug, Ladybug, now in your dwelling;
Your house is all tidy and not so repelling.
Your bread in the oven smells homey and sweet;
We'll come and we'll visit and enjoy this nice treat!

Ladybug, Ladybug, your lesson learned well;
Attend to your home and happy you'll dwell.
You pray and you clean, you sing and you spin;
Your friends will all come, you'll invite them on in!

Virginia Shibler

Hark! Hark! Let's Go to the Park

Hark! Hark! Let's go to the park,
We'll have a picnic today!
No need to go to school or work
For it's a Holy Day!

Our Lady assumed into heaven;
Her body and soul met her Son!
We go to Mass, then celebrate;
We'll play with our friends and have fun!

Pat-a-Cake

Pat-a-cake, pat-a-cake,
Make the priest his dinner.
He's been working very hard;
And he is getting thinner!

Many souls to save has he;
People need him all the time!
He offers daily Mass for us,
As the bells begin to chime.

Pat-a-cake, pat-a-cake,
We get his meal all ready.
We will cook it in the oven,
Then take it to the rectory!

Miss Penelope P.

Miss Penelope P.
Invited us to tea!
We dressed in our best;
Our tie and our vest,
To see Miss Penelope P.

Miss Penelope P.
Had tea under the tree.
With the flowers blooming;
The shade tree looming;
It was lovely, we do agree!

Miss Penelope P.
Said grace before our tea;
With honey and cake,
And crumpets she baked;
We were all quite full of glee!

We thanked Penelope P.;
For the crumpets and for the tea!
We went our way;
Didn't forget to pray
For Miss Penelope P!

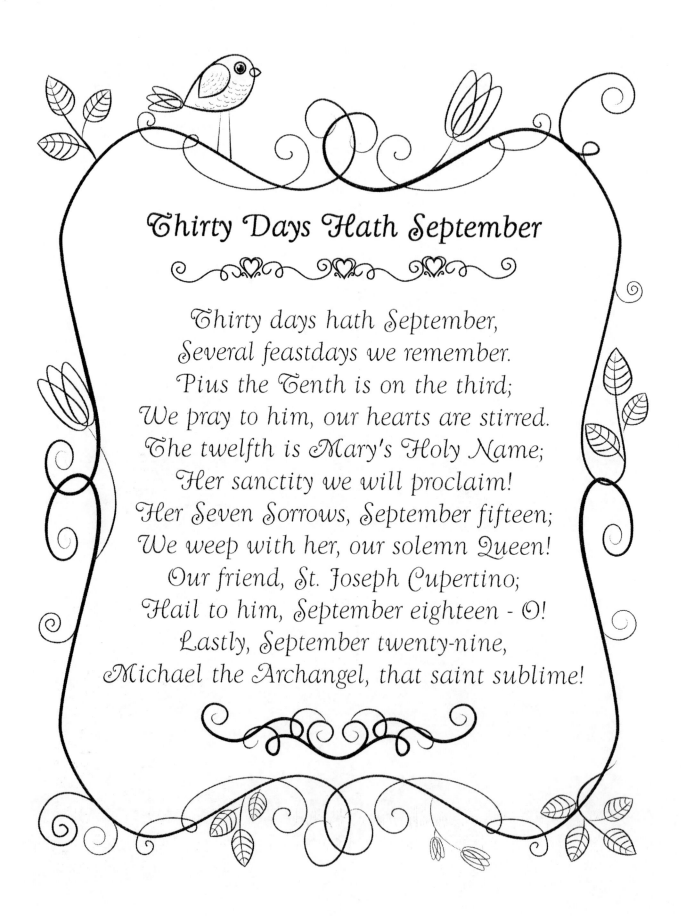

Thirty Days Hath September

Thirty days hath September,
Several feastdays we remember.
Pius the Tenth is on the third;
We pray to him, our hearts are stirred.
The twelfth is Mary's Holy Name;
Her sanctity we will proclaim!
Her Seven Sorrows, September fifteen;
We weep with her, our solemn Queen!
Our friend, St. Joseph Cupertino;
Hail to him, September eighteen - O!
Lastly, September twenty-nine,
Michael the Archangel, that saint sublime!

Ding, Dong, Dell

Ding, Dong, Dell,
Ring the doorbell.
Can Susie come and play?
It's lovely out today!

She will come soon,
But because it is noon,
The Angelus we'll pray,
To help us every day!

A Touch of Paradise

I love my pretty flowers,
So delicate to the nose;
St. Agnes sends a lily,
St. Theresa sends a rose!

The humble little violet,
The majestic sunflower too;
Each flower is a symbol
Of God's love for me and you!

We'll pick a small bouquet,
Put it in the vase so nice;
Set it in front of Mary;
A touch of paradise!

Baa Baa Black Sheep

Baa Baa Black Sheep, are you coming home?
Yes sir, yes sir, far away I roamed!
I spent all your money, I did go astray;
Please forgive me, Father, allow me to stay?

Baa Baa Black Sheep, my arms are open wide.
Yes, I will forgive you, please don't backslide!
You'll go to confession, we will call the priest;
We'll kill the fatted calf and all have a feast!

The Hobby-Horse

I had a little hobby-horse;
I rode on it all day!
It pranced and danced and clippity-clopped;
Such fun it was to play!

My mother called me to my chores;
I set my horse aside;
I did the dishes, swept the floor,
Then back again to ride.

My sister saw my hobby-horse
And hopped upon its back!
We agreed we'd take turns,
Galloping down the track!

Visiting at St. Ives

As we were visitng at St. Ives,
Father O'Reilly also arrives.

When he enters the room we all arise,
And greet him with our smiling eyes!

We sit down to tea at St. Ives
And chat with Father, good and wise!

Sitting on a Cloud

I've always wanted to sit on a cloud
Up in the sky so blue!
When no one hears when I think out loud;
Or sing a tune or two!

What a glorious time I'd have up there;
Floating above the land!
I'd dream and think with nary a care -
Oh! it would be so grand!

Then I would need to come back down
To my duties every day.
I'd think of the angels gathered round
In the clouds so far away!

Angels who would be doing God's jobs;
Not just floating in the clouds.
They're busy doing their duties, too;
Being Messengers for God!

Old Mother Hubbard

Old Mother Hubbard, went to her cupboard
To find some oil for bread.
The jars were no more,
For she was so poor;
She didn't know how they'd be fed.

Her debts were not paid, the old lady prayed;
They were coming to make her sons slaves.
Elisha came in,
Filled the jars to the brim;
With God's power the day he saves!

Nettie, Daisy and Lily

Nutty Nettie was sometimes naughty,
A little proud and slightly haughty.
Dizzy Daisy was usually lazy;
To get her to work would make you crazy.

Likeable Lily was typically silly;
When telling a story, Oooo...what a dilly!
When the three were together, Wow! What a team!
It would sometimes make you want to scream!

They didn't mean harm, but they were impish;
And their mischievous ways, they must diminish.
Their daily prayers, they still would say;
It gave them courage to change their ways.

So they grew and became more true;
Nettie, Daisy, and Lily, too!
They all turned out to be gentle and sweet;
To be with these girls was really a treat!

My Dear Angel

I love my dear Angel;
He protects me from harm.
He keeps me so safe,
When I lean on his arm.

I pray to him daily,
To make the right choice.
He whispers, "Be good,"
In his soft, gentle voice.

Glorious Fight

I do not like the Evil One;
He causes grief for everyone!
The day he fell from heav'n above,
Was the day he refused God's great love!

St Michael Archangel, strong with might,
Engaged the devil in a Glorious Fight!
Lucifer fell, St. Michael won!
A very sad day for that Evil One!

The Candle in Church

I lit the candle in church today,
And prayed for the souls gone by...
That they'd get out of purgatory,
And their souls to heaven would fly!

Eternal rest grant to them, O Lord....
I say with all my heart!
Let perpetual light shine upon them,
May their lives in heaven start!

The Little Flower

So sweet is the Little Flower;
Simple, yet full of mighty power,
In heaven's own majestic bower.

She looks down and always sees us;
Therese works to love and please us;
In the garden of Our Lord Jesus.

Life and all the problems it poses;
She is there right under our noses;
Answering prayers like petals off roses!

St. Raphael, Pray for Me

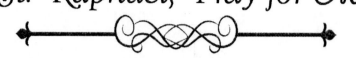

St. Raphael, please pray for me;
I'm traveling to Grandma's farm.
I'd like you to help me get there safe,
And not come to any harm.

When I am there, I'll milk the goat,
And feed the chicken and ducks.
I'll frolic and play in the hay all day;
Till in bed, it's time to be tucked.

And when I need to travel home,
I'll begin the long, cheery ride.
As you helped your friend, Tobias, that
day;
St. Raphael, be my guide!

My Saintly Teacher

I went into the garden,
To catch a butterfly.
He winked at me and flew away;
Then fluttered to the sky!

I saw a little ladybug,
I watched her small and free.
She looked at me and seemed to smile;
Then flew off her little tree!

I saw a caterpillar,
Inching along his way,
He nodded as he looked at me;
And went on his merry way!

St. Francis is my patron saint,
He loved each tiny creature.
I try to respect them just like him;
My saintly, gentle teacher.

Princess Desmitty

Princess Desmitty didn't think she was pretty;
She wouldn't take a step outside.
Don't be so vain;
Offer up your pain;
You shouldn't have so much pride!

Princess Desmitty, it is quite petty
To worry about your face.
Put your pride on the shelf,
Quit thinking of yourself,
And your heart will reflect God's grace.

Princess Desmitty, go out in the city,
God's kindness you can bring!
Though everyone flatters,
It's the **heart** that matters,
His Love is the important thing!

Princess Desmitty, overcame her self-pity;
She went out to her people that day.
She gave to the poor,
The sick she cared for;
Her people loved her in every way!

104

Little Miss Muffet

Little Miss Muffet,
Decided to rough it;
Knelt straight and still at prayer!

Along came distraction,
With its strong attraction;
She didn't fall for the snare!

Spin! Spin! Go the Wheels of the Bike

Spin! Spin! Go the wheels of the bike,
As Father goes cycling by!
He's in a hurry, he cannot stop,
But he smiles, waves and shouts, "Hi!"

Spin! Spin! Go the wheels of the bike;
Father must not be late!
Time for confession, the line is long;
His parishioners won't want to wait.

Spin! Spin! Go the wheels of the bike,
As Father makes his way back.
He takes his time, there is no rush;
So he stops to visit and chat.

Casey Truelove

Two Boys of Kilkenny

There once were two boys of Kilkenny;
They each had a jar of tenpenny.
It wasn't a lot;
They thought and they thought;
Of things they could buy,
With their scant supply;
To town they would go with their pennies.

The two young boys of Kilkenny,
Walked to town with their tenpenny.
They plodded their way;
St. Christopher they prayed;
To protect their travel,
On the road of gravel;
For miles to go, they had many!

The two young boys of Kilkenny,
Arrived in time a-plenty.
They were not spendthrifts;
They bought two small gifts;
Some treats for a snack;
Then started on back,
And prayed for their trip to Kilkenny.

God's Four Seasons

Spring is arriving, the weather is warm;
Sometimes it is lovely, sometimes it will storm!
We watch as the grass and the flowers do grow;
The creeks start to rise and they begin to flow.

The summer comes quickly, we swim and we play;
But sometimes the heat overpowers the day!
The flowers get thirsty and we are parched, too!
We water the blooms, then eat the berries we grew!

Then there is fall, with its welcome cool air;
It's a little chilly, so our sweaters we wear.
We carve our pumpkins, we play in the leaves;
They sail and they glide and land in the eaves!

Now winter has come with its cold, crisp feel;
We frolic in the snow, with joy and with zeal!
We cuddle up to the fire, when it's too cold outside;
We drink our hot tea, and put our playing aside.

We thank God for the weather, He gives it to us;
The four seasons change, and sometimes we fuss.
We must keep in mind that He knows what to do;
In spring, summer, fall, and in winter, too!

Hush, Children

Hush, children, my children,
I pray you don't talk;
'Tis time for the Mass,
Where our King feeds His flock.

Hush, Children, my children,
You must kneel so straight;
Your eyes on Jesus,
As you pray and you wait.

Hush, Children, my children,
Jesus is here!
He speaks to our hearts;
We listen and hear.

Shhhh.....

Shhhhh....

Protect Me

Sacred Heart of Jesus, be my life;
Immaculate Heart of Mary, be my love.
Guide me through the day,
As I work and play;
Protect me with Your grace from above!

God's Sweet Earth

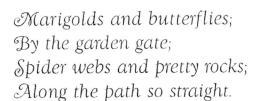

Marigolds and butterflies;
By the garden gate;
Spider webs and pretty rocks;
Along the path so straight.

Ladybugs and daffodils;
Growing by the grass;
Dragonflies and twinkling dew;
Sparkling just like glass.

Little snails and violets;
Sprinkled along the way;
Sunflowers and busy bees;
Brighten up the day!

Grasshoppers and dandelions;
It makes me want to sing;
I smile in awe at God's sweet earth;
And thank Him for everything!

My Hard-Working Dad

Lord, cover me with Our Lady's mantle,
And with Your Precious Blood;
For I am going to work today
With my dad and his friend, Bud.

We work in the heat and in the cold;
For Dad is a hard-working man.
I go with him to work each day,
And learn everything I can!

Little One, Little One, Where Have You Been?

Little one, Little one, where have you been?
I have been praying to Mary, Our Queen.
Little one, Little one, what did you say?
I asked her to guide me and love me today.

Little one, Little one, where will you go?
I'm going outside to play in the snow.
Little one, Little one, may Susie please come?
Yes, we will go and play and have fun!

Little one, Little one, you're kind and good;
An example to all of fine childhood!
You pray and you play, with a joy that is true!
You trust your Queen who takes care of you!

My Friend, Duck

What do you suppose?
My duck nibbled my toes!
Then what do you think?
He wanted to get my drink!
He took my little glass,
And swigged it on the grass!
I could have got real mad,
At my little comrade.
His impudence I forgave.
But I told him to behave!
He sincerely begged my pardon,
As we played about the garden!

There Was an Old Woman

There was an old woman, who carried a basket;
Each day she went to the temple to pray.
Why she was going, I didn't dare ask it;
She seemed so intent, as she made her way!

"Old Woman, Old Woman, Old Anna," said I,
"Oh whither, Oh whither, Oh whither you go?"
"I will see the Lord before I die,
And when I see Him, I will know!"

One day They came, Mary, Joseph and Him,
Old Anna saw them, and bowed her knees!
"I'll tell the world, though my eyes are dimmed.
He finally came, to save you and me!"

Three Children

Three children turned to worldly ways;
For fun they went in search;
They turned to sin and did not care;
They wandered from the Church.

Oh, had these children learned to pray;
And had they listened well;
They would not be in dire need;
Their souls almost in hell!

Ye parents who have children dear,
And want their souls to thrive,
If you would keep them safe and sound,
Then keep the Faith alive!

Little Robin Redbreast

Little Robin Redbreast perched upon a tree,
Along came a worm, he ate it with his tea!
Down came the snow, it's cold in the storm;
Not Robin Redbreast, his feathers keep him warm.

Little Robin Redbreast, God takes care of him
He's arrayed in glory, even more than Solomon!
God takes care of Robin, looks after him galore;
God takes care of me, and loves me even more!

Hickety, Pickety, Black-Robed Nun
-Becky Melechinsky

Hickety, Pickety, black-robed nun,
She prays hard for everyone:
For ladies and gents and children at play;
Her heart is devoted to God, night and day.

Hickety, Pickety, let's have fun;
Let's be holy, like the nun!
In all our work and play each day,
We'll turn to God often, to think and to pray.

St. Isidore, the Farmer

There was a holy man,
Who worked on the land;
He would come to his work often late, late, late,
You'd think this was bad;
But his boss wasn't mad;
For his work had been done first rate, rate, rate!

One day the boss did see
Work done by angels three,
While St. Isidore was at morning Mass, Mass, Mass!
All grew to love the saint;
No one had a complaint;
His work was finely done, every task, task, task!

Seven Sacraments

God gives us Seven Sacraments,
So that we may live in grace.
It's our way to get to heaven,
Where we see Him face-to-face!

Baptism takes original sin,
And casts it far away.
On our head is poured the water,
Our good Godparents will pray.

When we get older we may sin;
To **Confession** we must go!
To have our sins washed away,
And make our souls as white as snow!

A glorious day; the best in our life;
Is when we receive sweet Jesus!
Our **First Communion** is very special;
In our heart Our Lord will teach us.

We must be a soldier of Christ;
In His battle we'll be strong!
We receive our **Confirmation**;
In our heart there is a song!

We love someone and we get married;
What a great and special feast!
We receive the **Sacrament of Marriage**,
And say our vows before the priest.

Or Maybe God is calling us;
He will show the time and hour.
He wants us to be His special priest;
Holy Orders gives us the power!

Now it is time to see Our Lord;
We must be ready to die.
Extreme Unction is the grace we get;
And into His arms we fly!

God's Seven Sacraments are such a gift;
We thank Him every day!
We are faithful to His Catholic Church
And gather graces along the way!

My Days of the Week

Every day is fun,
I like each one!
I never get bored,
I do my chores.
Then I go to play,
For some of the day.
Then prayers at night
And tucked in tight!

The laundry is on Monday;
It's a ship-shape, do a ton-day!
On Tuesday we clean the kitchen;
Scrub and scrub, we will all pitch-in!
Then there is the Wednesday;
It's clean the barn wherein the hens lay.
On Thursday we need to clean the yard;
We like to do it, it's not hard.
On Friday we must dust and sweep;
Stations of the Cross before we sleep.
Saturday we gather the wood;
Then say our prayers, as we should.
Sunday is the very best of all;
With God and family until nightfall!
Each week we have our ups and downs;
I take them with smiles, and not with frowns!

Three Bees and One Bear

Three busy bees flew through the trees;
Buzz-dee-buzz, hum-dee-hum, high ding doe.
They were working while the sky was sunny;
Gathering pollen to make their honey;
Buzz-dee-buzz, hum-dee-hum, high ding doe.

A little fat bear, strolled without care;
Grunt-dee-grunt, hum-dee-hum, high ding doe.
The honey he found inside the tree;
He started eating with gusto and glee;
Grunt-dee-grunt, smack-dee-smack, high ding doe!

The bees were upset, no honey to get;
Buzz-dee-buzz, grrr-dee-grrr, high ding doe.
They scolded the bear, said he had sinned;
He should always ask, for honey again;
Buzz-dee-buzz, tut-dee-tut, high ding doe!

Commandment seven, helps us to heaven;
Buzz-dee-buzz, hum-dee-hum, high ding doe.
"Thou shalt not steal" the bear did break;
Other's things we must never ever take;
Buzz-dee-buzz, hum-dee-hum. high ding doe.

The bear was quite sad, he knew they were mad;
Grunt-dee-grunt, sniff-dee-sniff, high ding doe.
He was a sheepish and sorry bear;
He wanted to show them that he cared;
Grunt-dee-grunt, hum-dee-hum. high ding doe.

The bear came back, a pack on his back;
Grunt-dee-grunt, hum-dee-hum, high ding doe.
He opened it up, spread out a nice tea;
Goodies he brought, for the happy bees;
Buzz-dee-buzz, hum-dee-hum, digh ding doe!

Benny's Britches are Falling Down

Benny's britches are falling down,
Falling down, falling down!
He's too poor to go to town;
Oh! dear Benny!

We'll mend his pants so he can play,
He can play, he can play.
God teaches us to help each day,
Oh! glad Benny!

My Morning Offering

Every sunny , brilliant morning,
When the weather's nice and warm;
Every misty, rainy morning;
When its cloudy, going to storm;
It doesn't matter what the day;
Each season, work or play;
I say my Morning Offering
To get graces all the day!

Nighttime

It's nighttime now, I must go to bed;
I see the stars winking at me;
My parents will bless my forehead;
Then I go and brush my teeth.

A bedtime story is next in line;
I snuggle close to Mom just right.
She reads to me, we talk and laugh;
But now it's time to say goodnight.

I dip into the holy water font;
And ask for blessings on everyone;
I kneel by my bed and say my prayers;
And hop in bed when I am done.

I have tried to be a very good child;
And not cause my parents sorrow;
I ask Our Lady to watch over me;
And help me again tomorrow.

Nightime is so pleasant and sweet,
When close to Jesus we do keep.
I sink into my nice soft pillow,
And smile as I drift to sleep.

ABOUT THE AUTHOR

Mrs. Leane VanderPutten lives in rural Kansas with her husband of 30 years. She is the mother and grandmother of 11 children and 21 grandchildren....and growing.
Her family is devoted to Tradition within the Fold of the Catholic Church, homeschoolers, with 5 children still at home.
Their family life is lively, full of faith and joy!

For more copies of Catholic Mother Goose go
to www.finerfemininity.com
or email vinceandleane@earthlink.net

Contact:
Leane VanderPutten
8222 NW Arn Road
Rossville, KS 66533